A Life in Pencil

Ghada Kanafani

Ghada Kanafani

BAKSUN
BOOKS

Baksun Books
1838 Pine Street
Boulder, Colorado 80302 USA
303-444-1886

First Printing, September 2005
ISBN # 1-887997-58-X

Printed in the United States of America
Set in Garamond
Production by Arwa Hurley
Cover Design by Nuha Sinno, salam42@earthlink.net

www.ghadakanafani.com

Funded in part by the Boulder Arts Commission
and the Rocky Mountain Peace and Justice Center

ACKNOWLEDGEMENTS

My daughters, Arwa, Sara and Laila without whom life is not worth living. The first to read my work. Mark, the son I never had, whether he likes it or not. Sean Farid and Maura Najah, my grandchildren, who brought happiness, new beginnings and the bridging of the distance.

Amal who embodied hope, the assurance of life itself and the dignity of the roots: still standing unmoved, regardless.

I thank Jennifer Heath, who was the first to give me unconditional support and venues to read and publish. Jennifer, who spent endless hours thinking of and finding ways to make sure my voice is heard. Virginia (Badya) Lucy, the editor who drove hours on end for our Friday "dates," spent reading, editing, typing, eating....with occasional tears. Nuha Sinno, my friend the artist, who was a companion, from afar. For all the hope and encouragement through the years, and for her persistence and devotion.

Ghassan and ... who forever are alive in my memory.

The extended family of choice, on both ends of the choice, and the globe -- "you know who you are." You made all the difference just by being there.

Ghada Kanafani

PREFACE

Like wet eyes about to weep, these poems are hanging
between life and death, home and a denied home. They
are only sketches of what life has left in me and with
me, always in pencil.

When life happened, I was already at a loss; my homeland,
people, our collective memory and shared experiences. My
life-long companion has been the struggle for justice for the
individual, the people, and the cause.   My life experiences
left me bleeding most of the time. At best, they left me
with dents full of sorrows, loss, alienation, and a continuing
struggle for a place.

I left a country that was not mine, lived in countries that
were not mine, and draped the flag of surrender around
myself. For fifteen years I abandoned my self, my name, and
my writing. I felt the guilt of surviving and of having the
luxury to tell my stories while masses of people were being
denied even their memories by targeted assassination, mas-
sive killings, censorship, or by simply being dismissed from
the "official" history.

The longing for my homeland and the struggle to keep my
people and their stories alive is now, and has always been, my
post, my base, and my direction. My homeland and its peo-
ple are present, if not in person then in memory and in the
little objects of home we simply carried into our exiles,

through wars and fires, to refugee camps and continents far and near.

I am confident that these memories will live, if not for ourselves then for our grandchildren and generations to come; and if not now then, surely, later.

People came to my life. Some stayed with me and offered me a home. Others left violently, or gracefully. Trails of hurt and trails of love paralleled my veins. I can't help but thank them all for a life that is still going on, even for the pain that taught me to love more.

I will go on writing and living my words, coloring the darkness of our lives the same way I wear my most flowery outfits in the middle of bitter cold winter, anticipating the Spring.

G.K.

To Najah and Farid, my parents:
a smile that pierced the tears,
a home in spite of exile,
in a world that denied us home.

My Life in Pencil
(to Jennifer)

early enough
I learned about life
that's why
I always write
in pencil.

"Lower Your Eyes"
And i Did

"lower your eyes".
i was little
"always keep them low".
and i was little
"lower your eyes"
"lower your eyes"
"lower your eyes"
until i diminished.

I have to rip myself
from myself
to "look up"
to "face success"
to "look you straight in the eye"
to tell you "you are a liar"
to tell you "I see through you"
to tell you "ENOUGH".

"lower your eyes".
and i did
until i diminished.

too late for me now
to be "disrespectful"
too late for me now
to "take credit"
too late for me now

to "be visible"
too late for me now
to "say what i want"
to "say what i feel"
to "say what i need"
to "say what makes me happy"
to say "what makes me sad".

Only by sheer magic
like the magic carpet
I soar high
above the heads
not under the feet.

And,
for a few magical moments
I am
where I should be.

As for the rest of my life
i am lowered and lowered and lowered
like a corpse on its way to the grave
not all the way down
the opening not fully shut

i am just being
lowered and lowered and lowered.

Afternoon in a lifetime

Walking down crowded streets
like a tender breeze
in the middle of dry heat
thinking only of yasmeen.

Yasmeen and you
gave me one magical afternoon
in a lifetime of loneliness.

So much I longed for yasmeen.
I picked the buds
one after the other; they
yielded to my touch.

The yasmeen tree,
the shade, the scent,
a big sky of bright green
and scattered white stars.

Pink long drops of beauty
soft and tiny
gathered in my cupped hands.

My trembling hands took
a needle and a white thread
to lightly pierce each bud.
The needle traveled smoothly,

like a paper boat sliding
in a cool stream
trying to catch up with
the child holding the string.

A beautiful yasmeen necklace
with a knot white and secure
napped in a damp white kerchief.

Yasmeen's rising scent
invites me and says, Now.
I unfold the kerchief
yasmeen fragrance pours over me.

I wear the necklace
slide the kerchief
between my breasts.

Yasmeen carried me all afternoon.
Transformed to a beautiful woman
sliding through crowded streets
like a paper boat in a cool stream.

Yasmeen and you
gave me one magical afternoon
in a lifetime of loneliness.

Body

Tonight I borrowed your body,
the body that has so many lives.

I needed a body, other than mine.
I needed a body, that can pretend--

a body, that pulls a life of its choice

like a magician, from a hat
so easy, so smooth, so surprisingly magical.

I borrowed your body tonight
just to get me through the night.

I will return it tomorrow.

See? My body died on me.
Since then, I am either a beggar or a thief,

but never body and soul.

Marbles

Very few girls were allowed,
it's a boys' game

but,

I loved the bursting
colours trapped in glass.

Most of all, I loved
the scratched ones;

they've been around
and they win you the game.

Tahboosh was the master;
Tahboosh the whole,
the beginning and the end.

Hasan Sabi. Tomboy.

And,
I was in!

Then came the real game,
the men's game,

Ukht er-rjal.

I was promoted from
a tomboy to a
sister of men,

but,

women, most women
outgrow these games.

Their real game is to exist
not in relation to boys or men.

Women, most women,
frustrated and bitter
get in, straighten the records

and leave.

But,

men, most men
invent wars instead
and play women for marbles;

collect them, show them around
keep the shinier, discard the scratched.

And, yes,

they can't deal a winner,
they can't deal a whole;

after all,
they are after a hole.

And
Tahboosha is alone,

paying the price
of being complete
of being the beginning and the end.

A Princess

Take a princess, the one with the
most obvious power, the one with
a presence that dazzles all.

Take her, and no one else,
she'll make you look good;
she'll add to your charm. Then,
alienate her.

Take a princess
looking for life and hope, or
full of pain and despair. It doesn't matter--
she's a princess all right.

Tell her stories of love,
promise her kindness;
listen to her, like you've
never listened before.

Take her innocent trust.
Take her generous offerings,
take her silence, silence of the untold,
take her unconditional love.

Allow her a dream
of peace,
of deep blue seas
of finding place.

Don't tell her
she's an occasion;
don't tell her
she's a stop on your way.

Don't tell her you're a tourist,
don't tell her;
just don't.

She has been there before.
You killed a dead princess.

Returning?

You awakened in me a life
i had buried slowly over the years.
i was astonished when you
called me by my name,

and asked
why i don't use it any more.

i was astonished when
i faced the distance.
How am i to introduce you
to the self i have become?
Will you ever understand?

i love my name
when said right,

i need the distance to shrink.

will you wait with me
until I return?

Mummy

Wrapped from head to toe,
fully drained,
and it hurts...

Scarred all over,
and it hurts…

Buried deep down,
nothing to sustain me,
no honey, no wheat…

Buried deep down,
nothing to adorn me,
no gold no silver…

Buried deep down,
nothing to comfort me,
no sacred words, no gods…

Sealed shut,
no heart beat,
no tear…

Dark,
and frozen pain,
and frozen scream…

Don't unearth me.
Don't unwrap me.

Nothing more is left
but the scars
and nowhere to go.

Thank you

Thank me for a cup of coffee or a cup of tea,
thank me for an invitation or a call,
thank me for driving you around.
Don't thank me for loving you,
and don't thank me for my heart's gifts.

Thank you is for strangers, acquaintances
and I am neither.
When I love you, you become part or me,
do I ever thank myself?

"Grateful" to know me? I was hoping for
"happy" maybe "nice"
or better "lucky."

Grateful reduces me to "other,"
takes away from me
the chance to belong.

Teta and *Jiddo*

How do you feel now,
that you're a grandma?

Why the question?
How do you feel now,
that you're a grandpa?

Now, I have
a measuring stick of
a grandchild, who

will grow older inch by inch
day by day.

And
I will grow older
wrinkle by wrinkle
day by day.

I guess I feel old
wondering what to do
with the rest
of my leftover life.

So, how do you feel now,
that you are a grandma?

I feel happy.
Just happy.
Can't you tell?

Your question
is more about you.
A man, becoming a *jiddo*,
more than me becoming
a *teta*.

See,
when things happen
they happen to men;

instead,
when things happen
they just happen,
and that's that.

What happened to me?
Nothing.
I happened to you.

Sea

(to Mansour)

I miss you, sea.

I beg serene lakes
for blue, for waves;

I miss you, sea.

I beg raging rivers
for crystals, for rays;

I miss you sea.

I beg people's eyes,
look at the sea and think of me;

I miss you, sea.

I beg his blue eyes
for no tears, no goodbyes;

I miss you, sea.

I beg clear skies
for you everywhere

but

you're nowhere.

I miss you, sea.
I miss you, sea.

Waiting

... and when the moon
was complete,
it hid behind
the darkness of a cloud.

A star peeked from
the dark of darkness.
She sent her shine to
my eyes.

A moment of hope.
A moment of life.

And I will go on
waiting for the
moon.

To Sean

I am so happy Sean. I am just happy.
Now, I am part of a new life, a new beauty--

I guess you created me, a teta of your own.

I love the way you peek at me
from Arwa's embrace,

figuring me out:
First, I am a stranger
you give me indifference
and dig yourself back into your mom.

Then, I am a familiar face
you give me a smile
and plant yourself back into her arms.

I love the way you're hypnotized
when I feed you,

figuring me out:
        am I a boob with a spoon? A feeding toy?
Or an extension of some sort?

I love the way you
welcome back your mom and dad.

I love the way you know
where you belong, and
who belongs to YOU!

Seano, Thank you. I just love you.
and

I can't wait for you
to understand
what the hell
I am talking about.

Remember once
how broken words of worry
almost poisoned
the sacred questioning
of desire?

A Squirrel

Next to me the warmth
the hands the legs
that won't let go.

Next to me the belonging
the short-lived belonging
and the interrupted peace.

Next to me the face
the endless kisses
the wanting.

I took you all in
with my eyes closed.
My body drank you.

Stay. Will you?

Streams of caresses
and you drift to a sleep.
My eyes open when yours shut.

Once I wished for a gentle hand.
I watched rays of the sun
caressing the silver flow of a creek.

My hands my fingers
rays of sun
gently touched your silver hair.

Stay. Will you?

The sky gently wakes up
to its own morning
to its blue haze.

Your silver hair streams
through my fingers
my pearl painted nails.

Another short belonging
a perfect brush of harmony
stroked us, pearls and silver to the sky.

Perfection, I thought.
Beauty embraced us
into one.

Lazily you open your eyes
your green hazy eyes.
That's the world I want.

Stay. Will you?

"See the squirrel?" you asked
"Usually they're two
"they're only one today."

I saw your morning
with one squirrel
and a stolen belonging.

Stay. You won't.
But I saw your morning.
I saw the sky's dawn and mine.

Wine

Life packed in,
what is it called? Pandora.

Why did you open it?
Why? Why?
Why did you unpack me?

In your absence, and with
a glass of wine in one hand,
loosened buttons in the other.

Through your eyes,
I found me beautiful.
Through your memory,
I found a goddess.

My body took over.
Brushed my oppression
away.

No more, it said.

Another independent being.
A life sprouts from within.

You
shook my body out of me,

nourished it despite me.

Mirror, mirror on the wall.

I see shades of a woman.
I see faded beauty.
I see pale and frail.
I see bruises.
I see bruises.
I see bruises.

"Go away. Go away.
Shut your eyes.
I don't want me
in your eyes."

My body screamed, snatched away
my eye glasses, and
my magnifying mirror.

"You know me
like the palm of
your hand. You
don't need these."

My body moved away,
then suddenly
came back.

We danced.
We danced.
And sipped more wine.

That's when my body confessed
and made me
promise not to tell.

But, I love to gossip.
So, here it goes:

My body is waiting for you
like no other.

Longing is so fierce,
it rips the heart out.

The chest can't keep up
with the heartbeats.

The breasts, the lips are
numb with heat.

This body has gone mad.

All of a sudden
it stopped.
Asked me to hold it still.

And I did. I felt
sorry for it, and
shed a tear.

Now my body is waiting for you,
but would like to apologize for

a life

that left it dry,
bruised and old.

All it promises is
softness and warmth.

Not to worry body.
I will be with you.

I will slyly guide his
gentle caressing hands

away

away from the hurt, and
away from the stooping back.

And I promise to
protect you,

and if all fails
we know where to go.

Life also taught lessons.

New sprouts are beautiful,
spring buds and my body
are piercing to a new life.

I love the Spring, I love you.
I love the rain, I love
your delivering hands.

Still,
there will be no more wine tomorrow.

Yes,
There will be no more wine tomorrow.
There will be no more life tomorrow.

Only the wait,
only the wait.

And,
I put my wool socks on.
I slip me under the covers.

It's cold.
It's cold.

Long, Long
you insisted.
Long, long
you assured.

Your loving eyes,
your seducing smiles,
your delicate touches
convinced me.

Now,
like the sea waves,
they stretch to the farthest limits,
reach nowhere.
Defeated they retreat.

And
gentle caresses of
the playful wind
make my curls
long for your fingers.

I live you memory
in my present.

I hold you seed
to my future.

I hand you love
in people's paths.

I shine you light
in children's eyes.

I scatter you flowers
on mountain slopes.

I draw you circle
in moon's shine.

I drop you tears
in leaf's dawn.

I trace you wrinkle
in endless wait.

I weep you loss
in grieving hearts.

I scream you flood
in dried lands.

I bring you hope
to fertile promises.

Please don't fade.
I don't want to

leave you memory
in my present.

Salty Farewell

Now that I am caught between
two vague images of you,
it's much easier to slip away,
to let go.

I carried you through my turbulent life,
but when I found you,
you blurred all over again.

I smooth your erased particles off this page.
Gently.
The way I caressed your face.

Do you remember?

I smoothed your face, your eyebrows, eyelids, lashes.
Your salty beads covered the palms of my hands.
They trickled through my fingers;
some settled under my nails.

Salty Salty Salty.
My sweet, you turned salty.

Later.
I visited our beach.
A pillow of sand once dusted your hair.
Gently, the grains, in a blurred memory,

planted themselves, deep in your, then, very dark hair.
The same moments I was planting my kisses
deep into you and your memory.

Now.
Clear water runs over your skin.
How soon,
how immediate is your discarding of me.

In the now,
as in the distant past,
I keep you in every single pore of me.
I drink your salt. I keep you all over me.

I go back to my loneliness bathed in you,
blushed with a salty farewell.

Tumors

Letters to lovers
I never wrote,
each folded and addressed,

carried around,
banners of defeat.

Letters crept under my skin.
Lovers crept under my skin.

Tumors bulge all over me,
behind my eyeballs, behind my ears.

Tumors of lovers linger in me,
conceal my senses.

Tumors of letters, yet to be written.
Tumors of lovers, yet to be driven.

Only if,
only if...

Once My Butterfly
but, you thought
landing is deadly.

You barely touched beauty--
a quick peck, not even
a kiss.

Beautiful flowers awaited you
content with a peck.

                    Not me

Fly away--
unable to tell
the guiding, form
the burning light.

                    Without me

you're a moth,
forever burning
for home.

Deleting love

Never thought
in my wildest
          dreams

of seeing love
in Computer
          Language.

Distant.
Remote. Electronic.

Adored the Screen
lit with your
          love.

Longed for your voice.
Your words filled my
          eyes.

White. Green.
Characters.
          :) :) :)

Until,

I saw other faces
radiant with my
        happiness.

Cold and Distant
the way you to talk to
        Machine.

Searched for your
E-Messages.

Hard and steady
my palm cupped the
        Mouse.

And

        Delete.

You scrolled out
one line after the
        other.

My tears rolled down
one drop after the
        other.

Never thought in
my wildest dreams
of **Deleting** love.

But,

life makes everything
        possible.

And you became the
        other.

Distant.
Remote. Electronic.

When You Return

Give me a little more time.
Don't discard my shields
and open my being
without my defenses.

Don't leave me
scattered around
then calmly decide
that you're leaving now.

When you return,
give me a little more time
to collect myself,
to embrace it, to stand steady
behind my shields
before I go out to the normal.

When you return,
give me little seconds
of belonging and peace.

Hold me in your arms,
let me rest on your chest.

When you return,
remember that
you found me lost.

You invited me to life.
I forgot to tell you,
I am not lost,
I am practicing my death rituals.

I am tired of life.
Let me be.
Don't ask me to take care of me.
Don't tell me I deserve the best,
and wonder why I don't care.

I am tired of life.

When you return,
don't forget
I am waiting for
the latest news.

So many died.
So few I mistakenly thought
were still alive.
When you gave me
the latest news,
you did not stay long enough
to give me comfort.

So, when you return,
give me a little more time
for comfort,
is there any?

Give me forever.

When you return,
bring me a yasmeen necklace,
red poppies and za'atar.

Nothing is left of me,
but memories of the dead,
yasmeen scent and aborted spring.

Will you return?

Don't lie to me, or

one of me will find out
even before you know it.

See? I lived the examined life.
Like a butterfly, I kept
transforming to survive.

Yet, I carried in me my
passion, my driving force
toward a purpose not a destiny.

Look at me.
Look as hard as
you possibly can.

Do you see the lover?
The mother? The grandmother?
The worker? The poet?

Look harder.
What do you see?

The scars? The bleeding?
The cries? The defeat?
The dancing? The knowledge?

Look deeper.

Try. Try.
What do you see?

Can't see any more?

Now you know.

So don't lie to me
and don't work harder--
A perfect lie is just a bigger lie.

Just decide where
you want to be.

No, not with me ...

I know you.
One of me says, NO!

It takes one lie
and you're on your way,
away, away.

And
by the way,
don't lie to the
next woman around.

I Take It All Back

You are a mirage
not a balm.

Deep down, I knew
"it can't be true."

...told my doubts
not my love, not my love,

but, you proved me wrong.

I collected pieces of me,
my scattered self and life,

I collected and saved:
I saved me for you.

In a hurry I saved you my best;
then slowly I shed you, I shed me.

Numb with reality, I let go
of all that of me, of all that of you:
a past I longed to revisit with you.

Numb with reality, I let go
of all that of me, of all that of you:
a present I longed to live with you.

So we're not aliens.
So we're not aliens.

Again and again,
I have to leave my life behind
so I am not left behind.

Mercury

You don't walk
you slide. You smooth
your way around--
Mercury.

Sunshine on
dew drops
on deep green.

Thick silver
only charms
deadly if let in--
Mercury.

Slide away.
I mistook you for
dew drops.

Leave no trace.
Only a tear drop
on deep green.

Scratched your words out

Like the magnetic words
sticking to my refrigerator,
your words stuck
under my skin.

For a whole year
they scattered
with no meaning.

For a whole year
I waited.
But they stayed
uncomposed.

"Words that don't kill you
make you stronger."

Your words killed me some,
and with the ones that didn't,
I stained my nails.

A little dead.
With lots of scars,
free, I go on.

Shadows of love--
all that's left
moving on walls.

Shadows of love--
all that's left
scarring the memory.

Soon shadows disappear,
memories fade,
scars deepen.

The frail body slowly
drifts to peace, in
the deep scars of the earth.

Sieve

A harbor I am,
for departing ships.

With every departure,
a piece of me is taken away.

All I lived was departures.
and slowly I became a

Sieve.

Rusted holes became me,
and I became a circle.

I came to a full circle,
tight choking circle.

Harbors are but to harbor departures.

Long Distance

I miss you.
I miss you too.
And we laugh
our childlike laugh.

We should be together.
Yes. We should.

Your place or mine?
Definitely mine.
And we laugh,
our childlike laugh.

For how long we waited?
For how long we searched?
For how long we didn't know,
if you're dead or alive?
if I am dead while alive?

For how long were we separated?
Twenty some, maybe more, years.
Let's not... let's not...
We know what they were like.
Do we want to remember?
Your beautiful sweet voice invites:

"Come over here."
"Be with me."

My heart twists, bleeds
my eyes follow suit.
The stolen possibility,
the long ago stolen future.

I wish you were with me,
every moment. Every single moment.
Why don't you try? Just try.
And I catch my American self,
guilty of privilege.

Silence.
Silence on both ends,
the land and the mobile.

Silence.
Silence on both ends.
The far and the far.

That's where we ended
glued to the phones.

We,
the childhood friends,
the lifelong friends.

That's where we ended.
On two opposite sides.

Come over here. We say.
Be with me. We say,
didn't we wait long enough? We say.

If not here, if not there. Then,
let's pick a country that will give you
a visa.

Who will give a Palestinian a visa?

Let's pick a cloud.
Our final home.

Not much is left in our lives.
Let's pick a cloud, the one
who will not ask you for a visa,
the one who will allow you a tent.

We'll rain if we miss earth,
and evaporate if it rejects us.
We both know it will.

We'll live in blue, always in blue.
We'll let go, and the wind will blow.
Over treetops and doorsteps.
Will caress water and beautiful hair,
will tickle leaves and toes.

We'll be white and light.
And at night, we'll be unseen.
We'll play the stars,
sparkles for your hair.

The moon will give us kisses,
the way it always did.

My Palestinian childhood friend
my Palestinian lifelong friend,
don't rain without me,
don't evaporate without me.

Together we will write
the story of a cloud.

House Cleaning

Thoroughly cleaned.

It looks like a puzzle.

Full of retreating soldiers,
pictures of children,
none a refugee.

And the once house,
became a poem of erased poems.
Became my hand reaching a circle.

What is home but
a once dwelt-in poem?
Of blue and grey on white.

Don't shine your lights on me

Passing by at a speed
allowing but a glance.

Shining lights at a speed
allowing but a snatched hope.

Hit by speed and light.
I am left on the side.

The passing world avoids me.

Draining to the asphalt,
holding the last breath.

Losing sight, insides out,
losing hope, I start to give.

I surrender to pain
and hope for another jolt,
for instant death.

A stranger to myself
I am,
a stranger even to my touch.

My body
trembles in denial.
My skin retreats.
I jump from
under my fingers.

Is this me?

For so long
I molded me,
perfect for your taste,
now in my loneliness.

I am
a stranger even to my touch.

My eyes deny me.
I wander around,
looking for my face.

Mirrors forgot me.
Will I ever remember?
Who's going to remind me?

Pickled Words

Pick one, she said.

A see-through jar
full of folded words.

Pick one, she insisted
It was "mountains."

Pick a second,
she extended her arms.

My hesitant hand blindly
picked "plains."

Now, my confident fingers
reached in the jar of pickled words,

"Tragedy."

Invitation

An Invitation You Extended.
         To whom?
To me?

You don't know me.
Even I don't know me.

Until now, I thought,
I am broken, shattered.
Until now, I thought,
I can pick up the pieces.

Little did I know.
I am burned to

ASHES.

Take back your words.
Please, un-invite me.
Blow me away,

keep me only a memory,
a dream of yours.

Because the real
me is but
ashes attempting life.

A place I am headed,
a final place.
It surely exists--
the place I am headed for.

Doors closed in my face.
I imagined life behind them.
Now, they're closed
on silence and emptiness.

My endless longing for home,
led me to a
home without inhabitants.

I am locked between two mirrors,
between their faces.
I live images of life,
but not life itself.

I am locked in humanity,
without the humans.
I live love without lovers.

I am headed for a home,
vacuum of a home;
but it surely exists.

Sudden death
frightens me.
If I am to choose,
if I am to order my own
from the death menu...

It will have to be simple.
Cooked slowly, served on an earthy plate.
No side dishes, no drinks.
A flower on the side, would be nice,
but not required.

I prefer slow death.
A death that allows me
to process the life I had.

I like to take my time
to love the people I love
for a million times.

I like to tell them,
the stories of why,
the best I understood Why.

And I would like to love them
one million and one time, with
a flower on the side,
that would be nice.

And if I get my way,
pain will not matter,
because I can say ...

It would be nice,
if I have the time
to love you.

For a last time
really for a last time
with no regrets,
no tears.

I will be happy for
the wish that came true:
for the death that gave me
a chance life denied.

Only if I die
a slow death.

Only if I love you
one million and one times,
for the longest time.

...and nothing belongs to me.
Not my people,
not my homeland,
and despite the wounds,
not my sorrows.
Not in this world,
nor in another.

Beirut, 1967

My apologies

My apologies--
I was not ready
for your first visit.

So much, now I understand.
So much I should have done,
had I known.

My house was full of family,
I should have evacuated.

My land was full of crops,
I should have burned.

My water was plentiful,
I should have poured it out.

My songs were too happy,
I should have smothered those songs.

My children's laughter filled the air,
I should have silenced them.

All that and more
I should have done,
to prepare for your visit.

Or, was it a visit?

Had I known that
you're here to stay.
In My house, in My land,
claiming My songs and My air.

Had I known. Had I known.

I promise you,
I will be better prepared
for your next "visit".

Because you're leaving,
aren't you?

Mesa, Arizona

How many generations does it take
to make the "reservation" benign?

When did it start
to spell home? Does it ever?

Are we going to be in your shoes?
When?

Will we be saved from
becoming you?

Is that gourd your hollow body?

Are these your ashes rattling?
Or seeds of your future?
Allowed only to accompany
your heartbeat in a dance.
Only in a dance.

How soon will death
free us, to
the only peace we're allowed?

Playing only with leftover cards
we call identity?

Your place survived a bomb

Cold and naked. I walked around.
Once, life was alive. In this battlefield of the now.
Refuse is what's left behind. Including me.

I gave you roses. You chose still pictures,
Pictures of a past. Without me.

Your place and I survived a bomb.
Your place will recover.

I won't.

Collecting Home

An illusion of home, I short lived.

Why did you even offer?
Why did you invite me?

My hopes were your steps
into my home.

And I go on living,
an illusion of home.

Collecting scattered hopes, is all I can.
Collecting home, I cannot.

My home is my desperation.
My home is your deceiving.

He's a soldier today.
He's uniformly dressed.
Decorated with a machine gun.

He's running around the house,
"I am a soldier, I am a soldier."

I can't call him a fruit,
not even a product
maybe he's both.

Nobody knows.
Only the mom.
A Muslim caught
in the wrong place
by the wrong people.

Raped. Raped. Raped.

So, he's a soldier of what?
A fake, a make-belief soldier of what?
Of a fake, a make-belief independence?

He's a soldier of
a non-country,
granted independence.

You! The homeless refugee of parents.
You! The living unwanted in a non-homeland.

You! The survivors in a non-refuge.
Go ahead, celebrate a future killer;
a four-year-old, drilled into violence,
a four-year-old, shaped into a killer.

How could you?
How could you?

"It's independence day.
"He goes to school.
"You know."

Whistle

By chance, by mere chance
they see your desperation.
By chance, by mere chance
they see how far they've drifted.

All of a sudden,
they remember you.
You, who they kept aside.

A little guilty,
they blow the whistle.
And for a little while,
all is concern.

With calm resignation,
you wait for
their slow departures.
As little by little,
they push you aside.

You smile and wait,

for the moment when
by mere chance,
they blow the whistle
they call solidarity,
they call friendship.

September Floods

Streams of our blood
flow into one
bloodfall.

Floods of memory and of
memories-in-the-making
smudge my soul.

Forever. Forever
September
my failed escape.

On the way back
(to Brenda)

"How does the sky look in war time?"

The silence of the memory.

The sky burns
the clouds fight for a spot
not sure if they want to burn.

Sunset plays war games
burns in the west, the flames
seen to the north, to the south.

In the ever present past,
there was no sky.

The war has no sky.
Just the dark, the smoke, the soot.
Heavy suffocation.

The war has no sky.
Only sometimes it lights up
in the middle of the night.

The war has no sky.
Although some desperate people
look upwards. I don't know why.

The war has no sky.

"How about the moon?
"How does the moon look in wartime?"

Heart twisted. Throat froze. Mouth dried.
Poison ran through my body.

The moon was ugly at times.
So much hated.
It gave away our location.

The moon was lovely at times.
So long awaited for.
It gave us a path.

The war has a moon.
It's not your moon.
Just the knifing and the guiding moon.

The moon says that
not only the world, but
the earth fails us.

Always remember,
There's nothing romantic about the war,
not the sky, not even the moon.

Sorrows

(to Nuha)

It's not your fault
I lose sleep.

It's not your fault
my nights are
filled with your sorrows.

How many times
were you slaughtered?
How many times
were you imprisoned?
How many times
were you choked?
Were you silenced?
Tortured? Starved?

How many times
did you stop trying?

How many times?

Your throat is
a battle field.

And the nights?

Oh, the sound nights,
except for your sorrows.

Drowned in your own sweat.
Suffocated with your own breath.

Your mouth's full
with your own blood.

You're held down.
Pinned down.
Slaughtered.
Over and over.

My ears are tuned to
your sorrows.

I would offer you a hand,
but I am drowning
in my own blood.
Slaughtered
over and over.

On the fringes

Offered myself.
An eternal sacrifice,
my whole being
a humble offering.

But you kept me
on the fringes.

Offered myself.
To the last drop,
to the last nerve,
to the last sigh.

Offered myself.
To the last word,
to the last inch,
to the last glance.

But you kept me
on the fringes.

Here: take my ashes.
My last offering,
scatter them.
On the fringes of your being.

Memorial Day

(To Naomi)

A time to remember?
Did I ever forget?
I need fewer memories
of more losses.

Remembering is not an occasion
it's just there.

I lived my people's memories
until I had my own.

So, which ones do you want?

Of Haifa, my city in absentia?
Of an uncle I never met
holding bread in one hand
and a hole in his head, in the other,
bleeding to his destination?
Did the Zionist sniper know
'amu Khalil was getting bread
for his three little boys?

Of Beirut, my city in absentia?
Of jiddos I don't remember? My
grandfathers died in silence.
Of exile and a hope of returning home?

Of 'Akka, my city in absentia?
Of my mom, with a school
bag heavier than her own weight,
smuggling food and arms to the men
trapped somewhere, defending defending?

So, which memories do you want?
My own or theirs?

Of Beirut, my city of birth?
Of my three noble friends?

Of Nabil Hasan? The student.
One of the first to die
defending a city that isn't his.

Of Nabil? The photographer.
Photographs recorded his fall--
snap shot, snap shot, snap shot.

Of Nabila? The intellect, the humanitarian.
Assassinated at her doorsteps,
her young daughter a witness.
"Here's for all the food and medicine
you dared take to Palestinian refugees."

My three nobles.
My three peaceful nobles.
They died in print

in print, I knew about their deaths.
Memories of others or memories of my own?
Your place or mine?
Your memories or mine?

Of Hazmiyeh? The lunatic suburb.
Of Ghassan, blown up to pieces
hours before our scheduled date?
Did his Israeli killers know?
In his house I learned about
the humanity of their people.

Ghassan, forever my teacher
friend, protector. My ongoing
nightmare.

Of Hamad? The young child
with his little bucket.
Water was allowed to flow, then
bombs rained.
Did the Israeli army know?
Yes, they did. Yes, they did.
They turned the water on.

Of a nameless young man?
White T-shirt, circle of blood.
All I saw was his back, and
"Mama Mama Mama."
He was chasing after his screams.
Was he apologizing to her?

82

Was he asking her to make it go away?
Or just wanting to die in her arms?
I will never know. And,
the Japanese flag is forever
a desperate cry for a mother.

Your place or mine?
Your memories or mine?
It doesn't matter.

Memories of our graves,
mass and individual.

We die en-mass at home.
We die alone in exile.
Memories of graves, I
will never visit.
Memories of graves in absentia.

My enemy's memories?
Sorry, I have no room.

A day of remembrance?
Sorry, I can't afford.

Notes of Madness

I don't know why.
Is it a habit? Or
a necessity for
a retreating memory?

Why do I take notes?
To whom am I reporting?
No one.
Why then?

Why do
I take notes of madness?

When read later
my notes paint pictures
of chaos,
deadly chaos;

killings here; humiliations there;
hunger; filth; out-of-place dates,
names, professions, machinery,
Apaches, cities, villages, cameras.

Nothing to make sense of,
not the newspapers;
not the reports, seen or heard;
and not the live updates.

What's left, is scattered words.

Painting pictures of carnage,
of refugees and refugee camps,
of soldiers and children,
of soldiers and children--

pictures of miserable lives
in a frame of madness.

Not afraid enough to be silenced

I, I am Iraq.
I, I am Palestine.
I, I am the world masses.

Never again.
Never again.
We'll be your slaves.
Your slaves no more.

I, I am your own.
I don't want your
crimes staining me.

Don't I have enough?
I don't want to be haunted.

Savage screams
calling for war.

Fear engulfs the world.

Fear of the known:
shrieks of children,
wails of women
fill the ears.
Hearts, brains exploding.
Ruptured veins,

torn limbs, open wounds.
Blood, blood, blood.
Bewilderment, devastation, desolation,
burnt lands, gutted homes
and nowhere to go.

You smell blood.
Your primitiveness
takes over.
Kill. Kill. You want to
Kill. Kill. Kill.
You want to drink blood.

Controlling the dead, the hungry
is much easier.

Herding humans
is much easier.
When they're bombed
from all directions.
Bomb. Bomb. Bomb.

Listen? Understand? Value?
More than one truth?
More than one interest?
Unheard of.
All is foreign to you.
All is dangerous.

You just want to be
OBEYED

So, what's wrong with that?
No one is equal to you.
No one will ever be.
Nothing is above your wants.
The world is yours.
You are the world.
So, what's wrong with that?

You're the true keeper
of your interests, of course.
Your young ones?
They're to be sacrificed.
For you and only for you.

You are resourceful:
Even gods
are enlisted
for your war.

Scar future generations.
The killed and the killed.

What are you afraid of?

You can't imagine the world
without you.
You on top, of course.

Why don't you shape it
and re-shape it
according to you, of course.

What is it that you want?
Power? Control?

Can you imagine the world
with happy childhood for all?
With food and medicine for all?
With equality for all?

Can you imagine water?
Clear clean accessible.
Can you imagine art?
Colors where red is not haunting.
Can you imagine poetry?
Where words are pregnant with life.

I am tempted to simplify:
Can you imagine
education for all?

Can you imagine blue skies?
Bright stars? Light clouds?
Can you imagine a high moon,
Without your feet all over it?
Can you imagine?

You spread fear.
Fear of people seeing people.
Fear of losing what's not even yours.
Kill to keep what's theirs.
Kill to keep what's not even yours.

When did you become
the god of all?

Who assigned you the world?
Who gave you permission
to change red rose petals
into blood stains?

I, Iraq.
Women men children.
The dead the alive.
Land rivers and sky,
past present and future.
The memory.
The civilization.

I, Palestine.
Women men children.
The dead the alive.
Land rivers and sky,
The memory.

I, the U.S.A.
Women men children.
The dead the alive.
Land rivers and sky.
The memory.

I, the world masses.

WE are not afraid enough
to be silenced.

The world is a beautiful Mother-to-be.
Pave her path with red rose petals,

and step aside;
because:
All your fear
is not enough
to silence her.

Ghada Kanafani is Palestinian, born in 1948, in Beirut, Lebanon. She received a Masters degree in Philosophy from the Lebanese University of Beirut. She left Lebanon in 1984 and moved to the United States in 1985. She can be reached at www.ghadakanafani.com.